Signals

POEMS AND ESSAYS

Betsy Ellis Bowles

Copyright

Signals – POEMS AND ESSAYS

Copyright © 2014 Betsy Ellis Bowles. All rights reserved.

No part of this publication may be copied, stored in a retrieval system, or transmitted in any form by any means, electronic, mechanical, recording or otherwise, except brief extracts for the purpose of review, and no part of this publication may be sold or hired, without the written permission of the author except as permitted under Sections 107 or 108 of the 1976 United States Copyright Act, or through payment of the appropriate per-copy fee. Thank you for respecting the hard work of this author.

ISBN-10: 1494809168
ISBN-13: 978-1494809164

CONTENTS

Forward - vii

SECTION I. CONSEQUENCES - 1

Signals - 3

For a Moment - 5

Lost - 6

Carpet Patterns - 7

Fading Surface - 8

Reluctantly - 9

SECTION II. PROVINCETOWN - 11

Blue Ocean #26372 - 13

Poetry Class Off the Breakwater - 15

1856 – cod fishin' outa Provincetown - 17

Beach Glass and Bottle People - 19

Colorless - 21

My Good Fortune - 22

SECTION III. THE WAY OF ST. JAMES - 25

Betsy's Pilgrimage - 27

Made from Scratch - 32

SECTION IV. NEW ORLEANS: THE REAL WORK - 35

Fragile and Broken - 37

We get It! - 39

Reverend Mary Harrington Looking for Work - 41

If the Horse is Dead Get Off! - 44

SECTION V. WITH PAT - 51

Unfamiliar - 53

Landmarks and Timelines - 55

Big Memories - 57

Thin White Hospital Blanket - 59

Remembering Karen Barton - 62

Virginia at Christmas - 64

My Autumn Life - 66

Memorial Service for 9/11, Boston's City Hall Plaza - 68

SECTION VI. BENEDICTION - 69

Watch and Learn - 71

Lily Pads in Beech Forest Pond - 73

Prayer and Meditation - 75

ACKNOWLEGEMENTS - 77

FORWARD

Dear Reader,

These writings began as notes written on napkins in New Orleans, on bulletins from churches in Northern Spain and in the small place I call home in Provincetown, MA. There are some from a young woman, crazy, madly in love, and some from a deeply scarred young woman. Others I found in a collection I wrote long ago. I've always kept a detailed journal and found peace in writing about my experiences. Some writings here will allow you to see what was in my heart at the time I put pen to paper. Others are for humans that I love dearly.

There is no chronological order in these writings. Rather, they are ordered by their resonance against one another. I do know that I cared enough about the subject to explore it in my mind and in some cases, throw it into the sky, to let it swirl in my imagination. You might say of some, "It comes to no sound conclusion…." I say an obvious conclusion might have been too painful to follow.

As I reflect, certainly there was intervention in one or two of these.

For this I am extremely grateful.

SECTION I

CONSEQUENCES

But the cowardly, the unbelieving, the vile, the murderers, the sexually immoral, those that practice magic arts, the idolaters, and all liars - their place will be in the fiery lake of burning sulfur. This is the second death.

Revelation 21:8

Holy Bible – New International Version

Signals

> *"These are the healing cords that connect your spirit for healing and the truth of God."*
>
> *Phillip – My Master Teacher*

You linger lighter

   softer than the down feather

   once brushed on my breast

You hide in the tide's white foam

   bitter cold surprise on my heart and feet

You draw desire from my throat

   as my love sighs after love

   seeing flowers only seen with me

You sing the lonely futile flute

    you play my sad regrets

You cover me like the fresh lavender thrown

    at my wedding, delicious, erotic, stinging

Every grand gesture that blooms in me

    surely begins with you

Some are greater than I could dream alone

    Some whisper dark, too black to be heard

For a Moment

In an unfamiliar quiet

she lay close – still I felt alone

She sheltered me as best she could

Her eyes promised solitude

I buried my face in her long hair

And cried for you

She kissed my eyes to stop the tears

She kissed my lips to stop me

From saying your name

She made love to me

And tried to keep my heart from crumbling

Her naked body covered mine

The soft pain of infidelity

covered us both for a moment.

Lost

With eyes open I float in our empty bed

Will empty trees be gold before you return?

I imagine your hair as it covers my face

The music is here   then lost

The same melody when we made love

I cannot remember

how you kissed me when you wanted to be loved

Lost when I drown in you

Lost when I drown without you

In our empty bed

Carpet Patterns

Your carpet blurs before me

Am I green and you blue or

are we yellow and red?

Cool blue,

red passion

your amber fire

that lights my shadowed places.

I feel your absence clearly

I know our pattern.

Clarity seldom comes

to those who drink too much

and stare at carpets.

Fading Surface

we swam in deep emotion

attraction charmed me, chilled me

choked me

no explanation

you stole the shore

you waded willingly from my

flailing gestures   now,

my last breath gone, I float down

the light on the surface fades

like the taste of your skin

like the life I struggled to seize

Reluctantly

Before dawn, I slip from your bed

From the calm of your shadowed face,

Your breath's heat, the world we hide in.

I long to stay, to repeat our sounds,

To wait for burning daybreak to melt your

unwanted dreams of deceit revealed.

No solace, only endless, fitful nights for sinners.

We struggle against the sleep that keeps us

from making love….again.

I stagger, I stumble, betrayal

makes me weak remorse blinds me,

my breath stops. I fall

to my knees finally

I leave you.

SECTION II

PROVINCETOWN, MA

"Like Nowhere Else"

The 1970s marked Provincetown's rise as the gay and lesbian mecca and destination that it is widely considered today. It is a place where you can be yourself without fear of condemnation.

Provincetown Office of Tourism

Blue Ocean # 26372

It will ruthlessly heave these vessels to and fro, break them into pieces in its sandy or stony jaws, and deliver their crews to sea monsters. It will play with them like seaweed, distend them like dead frogs and carry them about, now high, now low, to show to the fishes, giving them a nibble. This gentle ocean will toss and tear the rag of a man's body like the father of mad bulls, and his relatives may be seen seeking the remnants for weeks along the strand.

Thoreau's "Guide to Cape Cod,"
Edited by Alexander B. Adams

One of many vessels, she rests today in a tranquil harbor

Uncertain of her next day out.

Her white stick-on letters barely visible through the rust.

Not sleek, but an irregular craft

Working and strong of serious intent.

Rusty chains, rusty wrenches,

Rust bolts and a large rusty spool.

Dirty plastic crates ready for fishes.

Once glossy with new paint, her battered hull

Seems wavering in its strength.

The Captain's features are irregular.

A dark, rusty man, too old for his years.

Irregular lines in his unshaven face, irregular teeth.

His torn tee-shirt and tattered, faded jeans

Possibly worn since Monday.

"I have maintenance"

Nine inch needles in his large thick hands

Link nets of green, black and orange.

He flings unwanted catch into the bay.

The pale pink guts glisten and sway on the surface.

"Sometimes six days, sometimes seven…

all depends on the weather…."

If his ancestors had been delivered to sea monsters

And their remnants washed on some shore,

He chooses not to say. The Blue Ocean

26367 rocks in the harbor

Uncertain of her next day out.

Poetry Class Off the Breakwater

The instructor says "name the colors you see."

I see you. Perhaps you remember crayon colors as a child.

The instructor says "write about darkness and sunlight and shadow."

Did bitterness replace light as your sight dimmed to darkness?

The retreating tide swirls in uneven channels

Leaving ponds that suggest the artist changed her mind.

Blue, no, gray-blue, no dark blue with silver shadows.

Do all your days seem dark blue to you?

There are a hundred shades of sand – amber, tan, yellow brown.

I will tell you how the grass, closely observed, is luscious lavender,

The dunes in the background ice the horizon.

Perhaps you recall a cake with bright icing that spelled your name.

They say there is a black underbelly to my breakwater town,

Forty overdoses and two deaths in one weekend alone.

Instead of that, I try to describe these colors, this view for you.

1856 – cod fishin' outta Provincetown

We walk down to Pease's Tavern on Tuesday nights –

John and me.

Captain Turner don't come – shackled to that big new house –

Maybe shackled to Miz Turner.

He got plenty of luck, that man, and smart as they come.

In April he walks up to get us – always takes John and me –

he's good that way.

We go out 900 miles – sometimes more. Captain can feel the spot.

'Bout fifteen men on the *Blue Ocean*.

John and me always fish first. Then we clean.

John's got the best knife for back-bones – a old ivory thing

from his Grand-Paw's Paw.

Captain's always the salter – faster than any man on any

one of them hundred ships out there.

We stop at sundown – I got a mighty bunch of pains by then.

Captain's always the counter – no sense not trusting Isaiah Turner.

We're the last ones to come ashore …

gets right nippy mid-September.

September 13th is the Miz's birthday – always home by then.

I made $55 – best ever. John made $58.

We ain't ever the high-liner. But Captain said 82,000 lbs. this trip.

At home $5 goes in the wooden box

for whiskey on Tuesday nights at Pease's.

Beach Glass and Bottle People

Very early this morning at low tide

I began my second season as a scavenger.

I was looking for the glass

that has washed itself to and fro

on this narrow stretch of beach

near the old shipyard, not far from our place.

Townies remember an apothecary shoppe here long ago.

Unwanted bottles of all sizes, shapes and colors

were tossed along the shore,

so they say.

I kicked aside broken shards

that once I would have stooped to gather.

Then, I dug. I bent down, searching

for a keeper. Something unique –

unusual in shape, deep in color or

maybe etched with a seafarer's logo.

Beneath a rotting pylon, facing up to me, there it was –

whole and intact, a frosty pale blue bottle

only two inches wide and seven inches tall

but smooth and unbroken,

- a perfect bottle from the bay.

There are people like my shards.

Some broken by sharp, external pressures,

some worn smooth by the monotony of daily trials

and some worn irregularly from within.

There are bottle people, too.

I wonder how they've made it so far,

what they've really seen, how they survive

and what they silently know.

Colorless

No color this early morning.

Gulls allow me to share their beach.

Dark grey legs and beaks,

medium gray bodies, light grey heads.

Grey green water, grey blue sky,

frothy grey white surf.

Colorless things come to mind –

a black and white photo of my Mother

in a black and white swimsuit,

her left hand provocatively placed on her hip,

her head tucked slightly,

a private knowing smile.

My Father kept the photo in his wallet

away from the fading light.

My Good Fortune

Early this morning I rode my bike easterly

along Commercial Street, past Snail Road and then north

on Route 6A out of Provincetown.

In my new biking shorts,

a thin nylon hot pink tank top, no bra –

who cares if someone notices my left breast?

I pedaled past rows of weathered condos that face the blue bay

past long stretches of dense pink wild roses, dingy lobster traps

and ships waiting to sail. Erotic

breeze through my shirt.

I speak to everyone on the road, "Good Morning"

"And Good Morning to you too!" She

is beautiful. Heavy set, skin the colour of dark chocolate.

In a long denim skirt, a Patriots T and flip-flops,

on her way to work. She stepped aside; I pedaled off

to play my day away.

My educated parents, my charmed childhood

with its pink bedroom in Virginia.

X-rays showing new cancer in my left breast.

I focus on my afternoon mosaic class —

will I select the right colors,

will I cut the glass correctly,

can I design something good?

I decide I like the reds and oranges the best.

I pedal on. Sun warms my face

and wind cools my skin,

what's whole as well as what's lost.

SECTION III

THE WAY OF ST. JAMES

People have walked this 800 km pilgrimage route across Northern Spain for over 1000 years. They walk as a profession of faith, as a form of punishment, as a means of atonement, or as way of acquiring merit. (It is believed, that in certain cases, the amount of time spent in Purgatory would be reduced to half)

Betsy's Pilgrimage - "The Way of St. James"

(September 20 – October 1, 2011)

This journey began for me in the summer of 2000 as I walked around the Lincoln High School track in my hometown of Winchester, Massachusetts. I was exercising my left arm during 29 days of radiation for breast cancer. While I walked I listened to Shirley McLaine's account of her spiritual journey on "The Way of St. James" also called "The Camino." She walked the entire 500-plus mile trek across Northern Spain.

I dreamt about the solitude of hours of walking, the serenity of the Northern Spain countryside and the fellow Pilgrims I would see on their journeys. I pretended to be a Pilgrim as Jack, my 4-year-old Labradoodle, and I walked on the trails in the Middlesex Fells. I hung a large photo of the walk's destination, the Cathedral of Santiago, in our studio in Provincetown. This was my reminder of this "once before I die" journey that I felt so compelled to take.

I was delayed several years by "life circumstances," but in September, we accepted an invitation to a wedding in London. "I will never be younger, I may never be more fit, and I may never be closer," I thought. Just for fun, I asked our travel agent to research plane schedules to Madrid and train schedules to Sarria, the beginning city. I also ordered my "credential" from the Americans on the Camino Association. Credentials must be stamped in hotels, restaurants, or refugios along the way to verify that the walk has been completed. I bought fast-drying underwear, two pairs of convertible pants and a Tilley hat. This was truly a case of "throw it to the universe." And as the universe would have it, it actually happened just the way I believed it would.

Early Pilgrims obtained their credentials from their home town church or Bishop and used the passport for food and lodging. Having the passport stamped along the way also enabled the Pilgrim to receive a Compostela from the Cathedral authorities at the end in Santiago. This document further proved that the pilgrim had in fact walked the entire way.

After the death of Christ, the Disciples were sent by him to every corner of the earth to spread the Gospel. James, one of Christ's first disciples, was sent to Spain. Over time, many stories centered around James, his ministry in Spain, his death and the early Christians who followed him.

Today, pilgrims stream up the Cathedral steps, then kneel and place their hand on the marble pillow imprint made by thousands of hands before them. The next act requires one to go up the stairs behind the altar and place your arms around the neck of the gold stature of St James. From there, Pilgrims follow narrow worn stone steps to the lower level when the remains of St. James are housed in a small silver casket.

Pilgrims travel light, carrying just a walking stick and scrip (knapsack) and a gourd for water. I carried 2 pieces of each type of clothing, three pair of socks. No contact lenses, no make-up, just toothbrush and paste, deodorant, mole skin for my feet and Tylenol.

The scallop shell has become an essential part of the Pilgrim's uniform. These large ridged shells were gathered on the coast at the end of the walk and taken home –another way to prove that you had done your work Today they are worn around Pilgrims' necks, tied to their knapsacks or dangled from their walking sticks. These are also the emblems of direction – used in all forms along the route to point the way to Santiago.

There were several guardian angels along the path when I walked it.

1-) Michael – the desk clerk at The Hotel Roma in Sarria who helped us map our first day.

2-) The Danish woman who lead us through the darkness to the pilgrim path out of Sarria.

3-) Monica – the woman in the gift shoppe in Portomarin who made sure our "mochilas" (backpacks) made it on to Ventas de Naron. She also sold "Jimmy" to me. This unique walking stick was carved by her cousin.

4-) The worker in the green emergency vehicle that took us to the hotel in Melide.

5-) The sweet woman in the countryside who had us wait by her gate while she ran into her house and brought out two huge red apples for us.

6-) The Inn-keeper's wife in Salceda who fed us so well – wood grilled pork and white wine.

7-) The silver haired woman in the Cathedral who told me, "I like your country"

8-) The German priest who copied the Pilgrim's Mass scripture from the big altar Bible for me.

9-) All the Pilgrims in all their different languages who said "Buen Camino" as they walked past.

10-) And last but certainly not least, the airline employee in Santiago who wrapped "Jimmy" in newsprint and plastic bags as she explained that "walking sticks fly free." She booked him from Santiago to

Madrid, Madrid to London, and London to Boston. He made it to me in Winchester – all alone and only 3 days late.

I could try to describe what I saw – the rolling countryside, the tree and stone walled paths, the Spanish hamlets, the silver eucalyptus forest, the many sacred places and the amazing Cathedral, but I did a picture book for that. The pain of my blistered feet and the broken blood vessels in my legs, my swollen hands and the aching parts of my body will not soon be forgotten.

As I walked, I frequently stopped and wondered how many feet had stepped just where mine were stepping. I wondered what burdens those pilgrims carried on their journeys. Why did they choose to walk? I tried frequently to be "in the moment" – all the while asking my personal guardian angel, "Exactly what am I to learn here"?

Mickey said she thought I was doing this to prepare for the next phase of my life. Perhaps I did it for all the Pilgrims who had walked there before me.

The Cathedral in Santiago is like no place I have ever been. The music, the incense, the Pilgrims and the magnificence of the building itself is indescribable. I do not doubt the reality of forgiven sins by the placing of one's hands in the handprint of the marble column or the blessing received by St. James while putting your arms around the statue's neck.

Not a day goes by that I don't think of that place and picture the Pilgrims there on their knees. It was Marianne Williamson who said, "Until your knees hit the floor, you are only playing at life." I believe she is correct.

So, what did I learn over nine days and 73 miles?

Will I tread softer on the earth?

Will I cling less to the material things in my life?

Will I love more sincerely, more deeply?

Will I sense the important things more readily?

Will I be a better Unitarian?

God, I certainly hope so!

My fellow Pilgrim and dear friend of 35 years, Lorraine May, could not have been a better traveling companion. I am thankful for her.

And thankful, beyond the beyond, for my spouse and the fact that she finally gave up the idea of putting a chip in my shoulder so she'd always be able to tell if I was still walking.

P.S. The only person I remember saying "TAKE ME WITH YOU" was Rev. Mary Harrington. She passed away from ALS in October of 2011.

Made from Scratch

How to use a recipe:

read the directions completely, prepare special utensils, assemble all ingredients —

do NOT alter the amounts. Assemble all equipment. Measure precisely, Mix precisely

Bake as directed. NOTE; Over or under mixing, especially in baking,

can give disastrous results

*Copied from my Mother's
Southern Ccookbooks*

1 cup Christianity

¾ cup discipline

½ cup kindness

½ cup honesty

Equal parts empathy, humility, trustworthiness, appreciation

Dash of accomplishment

Parents love to taste

The mother followed the directions

but the girl child was a disaster.

Father's genes were quite respectable – the timing was correct.

Beautiful chocolate brown eyes, vanilla baby skin.

But with age the ingredients began to sour.

Rebellious behavior got stirred in the mix.

Carving initials in her leg,

swimming in the off limits quarry.

Lying, cheating, stealing

were not the desired results.

Too much Jesus – not enough God?

Who's to say amid regrets.

The girl now bitter

knowing her mother followed

the directions she was given.

SECTION IV

NEW ORLEANS: THE REAL WORK

August 29, 2005
Hurricane Katrina, at one point a Category Five storm, caused $81 billion in property damage and left a death toll in the thousands. In New Orleans, the storm surge caused more than 50 breeches in canal levees and 80% of the city was flooded, with some parts under 15 feet of water. Approximately 85 percent of the residents of New Orleans were evacuated. 1,836 people lost their lives. 705 are reported still missing.

In 2006 Rev. Mary Harrington and I founded a 501 C-3 non-profit organization, Gulf Coast Volunteers for the Long Haul. Long Haul has spent over 39 weeks in New Orleans since Katrina. Our volunteers number over 300. We've worked on over 60 houses. We tutored the children of New Orleans in 6 schools.

Our motto is: "Helping rebuild their homes, their communities and their lives for as long as it takes".

Fragile and Broken

I have been thinking somewhat differently since our trip.

Stopping to categorize my thoughts, most can be grouped under two headings:

thoughts of things that are fragile - some tangible.....some intangible

thoughts of things that are broken - some tangible.....some intangible

I think a lot about the fragile feelings of the fifteen volunteers who made this memorable trip to help the survivors of New Orleans after Hurricane Katrina.

How fragile our feelings were – we cried quietly alone, we cried together in our evening de-briefing meetings and we cried in fragile moments as we physically embraced our fellow Unitarians.

Naturally, because of my work as a mortgage broker, I would think about the fragility of home ownership. I think it should be everyone's right to have their own home. Picture your house. Everything you own – in every room, everything from your outstretched arms down, moldy and soggy from days of being in toxic mud and water.

How fragile the poorly constructed homes were in winds over 140 mile per hour.

How fragile were items I saw like baby shoes, a sewing machine and a treasured photo album as they were swept away by a 20 foot wall of water. We don't know where they came from – just that they landed in a ditch of stagnant, yellow-green slime.

How fragile were the refrigerators as they floated from room to room.

How fragile were the moldy green and black splotched walls we took down and moved to the curb.

How deeply fragile was the sense of loss when a man chooses not to take his wife back into their destroyed home. To quote him – "It would kill her on the spot".

How fragile the levees were when the river water cascaded over the top and the city's fragile pumping system lost power and failed.

How fragile were the lives of the city's 500,000 citizens left homeless – a high percentage of them black, poor and children.

How broken is a system where it was impossible for a daughter to find her mother for 63 days. As the water rose, her mother was moved from a Hospice House to the local hospital, then to the jail, on higher ground, where she died. Ultimately her mother was sent to a morgue in another county with hundreds of other unidentified bodies.

How broken is the mentality of one community that would put citizens of another community in harm's way because of the color of their skin.

How broken is our country where every American does not feel deep compassion for the people of the Gulf Coast.

How broken are we, as citizens of the richest country on the planet, if we don't rethink our commitment.

A commitment that should be neither fragile nor broken.

January 2006

We Get It

You frequently hear us say

"You really have to see it before you get it"

After spending time in New Orleans the second time, I get it. I get a deeper sense of how tragically complex the state of affairs is there – one parish to another. The flowering pear trees are almost in full bloom but the yellow-green slime is as thick as it ever was in the ditches along the roads.

The ninth ward has a few less refrigerators along the curbs but the majority of the houses are still not repaired and vacant – the inhabitants of these houses had to move – maybe to Texas or Florida. The lots here are too small for trailers. Steve, a Unitarian man we met has finally put paneling on one room in his house but had to remove his damaged front porch in order to get a water line in for his new trailer.

In St. Bernard Parish, white trailers still pepper the long city blocks. The owners, with the help of volunteers, are still dragging out their refrigerators, soggy ceiling insulation, moldy carpeting, warped furniture and treasured items. In the small yellow brick ranch where I worked, a sweet woman asked if my volunteers would please find her wedding ring. We moved for three days through six inches of toxic water and mud with copperhead snakes and crayfish. We found two of the small glass elephants from her collection – unbroken – but not her wedding ring.

Over a third of the city's houses did not have flood insurance. In some cases there may have been a title or deed from three, maybe four generations back, but no one remembers. What will become of these small family homes where there was once a family crowded around the dining room? I know no amount of volunteers will be enough. Not enough money to rebuild. Not enough people returning. Not enough tax money. Not enough interest in rebuilding this city.

The mailboxes have not been replaced. Only one half of the traffic lights are operable. But some folks drink the water and some who have returned drive 25 miles to buy a pint of cream for their morning coffee.

How ironically complex is it that a psychiatrist can't make a living when the suicide rate increases every day? How complex is a system that cannot manage to get a trailer for a 92-year-old woman who just wishes to return to her neighborhood to die? Why is it necessary for twenty-eight city workers to be involved in placing one trailer on a lot for a family of four? And why does this take six months?

We get "there but for the grace of God go we."

We get what it is like to see and feel things that make you heavy of heart.

We get it – hurricane season is less than two months away.

January 2007

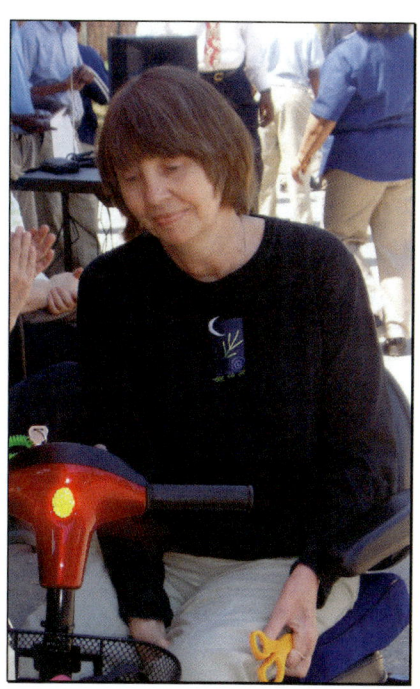

Reverend Mary Harrington Looking for Work

In January of 2007 Rev. Mary Harrington and I flew to New Orleans to assess the needs in the Seventh and Ninth Wards and plan the gutting and remodeling work for future Long Haul volunteer trips.

A portion of our recent trip was spent with Sister Maura O'Donovan, a wonderful, white-haired Irish nun from the now closed Catholic Church of the Epiphany. The church was the center of this seventh ward's "brown community." Now it's a familiar scene to us; block after block of uninhabited houses; some wide open, some with 4 X 8 sheets of dirty plywood hiding what's inside, and some ready for demolition. All still have the red status markings of information put there by the FEMA employees right after the water receded. On one front porch I saw the inspection date was September 13th, my 63rd birthday. I also saw ugly letters that spelled "Dead Dog."

It was on this trip that I met a Creole woman, Camille Pachon. Camille is a devote Catholic with a deep sense of her faith and commitment to her church and community. She works in a convalescent home to support her family and send her two daughters to Catholic school. She says her job taking care of twenty-three elderly people is difficult. Camille's family is the third generation to live on the corner of Frenchman St. and North Rocheblave Streets, diagonally across from the "Who-Dat" Tavern. Her clothes were worn but clean. She wore a grey sweater over a blue housedress and hot pink fuzzy socks with sandals. Her thinning brown and grey hair was pulled back to the nape of her neck. Her painful look was constant, her guarded smiles infrequent. I was immediately aware of how attractive she still is even after all she has endured. She had beautiful milk chocolate skin and dark piercing brown eyes. Her resolve is rock-solid. I began calling her the "most tenacious woman in all of New Orleans" – this made her smile.

Over the past 100-plus years, Camille's small house has had two small additions; one small bedroom for her mother, and one bedroom later for her son. After Katrina, the city denied Camille's request to tear the home down because of its age. The law claimed it had historic value and could not be razed. Standing on the inside with Mary, Camille and Sister Maura, I could see daylight between the plywood gaps in the walls. The sunlight from all the open spaces made weird patterns on the patched, uneven plywood floors. The baseboards showed extensive termite damage but the house had been gutted.

Her youngest daughter paints palm trees on pieces of wood debris from her house and gives these "pieces of art" to volunteers who come to help them.

A heavy coat of dust covered a table and three odd chairs that Sister Maura had found for them to use later. Camille explained that she was looking for one more chair so the family could sit for a meal.

Camille waited four months for an interview to request assistance from the government's Road Home program. It's now been two months and she's heard nothing. We agree to return in March to put up new insulation and sheetrock. I fear Camille's "restored home" may not be strong enough to withstand the next storm.

Camille, her daughters and her disabled husband now live in a FEMA trailer parked beside the house. There are two statues of the Virgin Mary outside the trailer steps; one small grey stone figure and another quite large one, cloaked in the common blue robe. The head had obviously been severed from the body but somewhat reattached. The only time Sister Maura broke down was in the telling of how the Seventh Ward families gave money beyond their means to install the stained glass windows for their now chain-locked sanctuary. Before Camille accepted our help, she wanted to know our Unitarian beliefs in reference to Jesus. It is very obvious that faith keeps these people pressing forward. I feel my faith might not be enough.

"Ike," the family pit-bull, wagged his tail and watched us from his 5 x 5 chicken wire pen between the FEMA trailer and the house. He has torn his bedding apart and from a distance it looks as if he is standing ankle deep in snow – quite a contrast to the brown grass, brown bushes and dead trees. People are not the only victims of Katrina. I feel an affinity with those people who would not leave their pets.

There will be a Congressional hearing in New Orleans today. The Senators will be seated in the big judge chairs and the New Orleans officials will all be seated on the floor. How could this situation remain after nineteen months? What will be done? Who will intervene? I think we have failed as a nation. I feel ashamed.

Mary and I found more work that we can ever complete. We agree to continue - "one house at a time."

February, 2007

P.S. Long Haul will return to New Orleans in March of 2014. I must ask Camille if her daughter's baseboard still needs to be installed.

If the Horse is Dead, Get Off!

In a bar, between connections on my flight home from my seventh service trip to New Orleans, I had a beer and cheered with other travelers as we watched the New England Patriots beat the Indianapolis Colts. That place, Charlotte International Airport, seemed a million miles away from the elementary school and playground on the corner of North Villere and Pauger Streets in the Seventh Ward. And that time, late Sunday afternoon on November 4th, 2007, seemed light years away from only two days prior.

The clothes I took had changed since my first trip in November of 2005 only two months after Hurricane Katrina flooded 80% of the city. My father's hammer and my heavy work boots stayed behind – no gutting houses on this trip. As on previous trips we slept on air mattresses in a Methodist Church. We cooked our own meals and ate along with other volunteers from Ohio and Virginia. Our focus before had been rebuilding. Around the city there are currently over 700 houses in different stages of disrepair.

Our focus this trip was the children of New Orleans – specifically a few of the 280 kindergarten through 3rd-grade children at the A.P. Toureaud Elementary School on the corner of North Villere and Pauger Streets. A.P. Toureaud was New Orleans's first black attorney and there is a large photo of him in the school's trophy case. He looks stern, refined.

Outside the school, next to every entrance, there are large, old white signs with rusty bolts that read:

WARNING:

ANYONE WHO COMMITS THE CRIME OF CARRYING A FIREARM ON A SCHOOL CAMPUS OR SCHOOL BUS

SHALL BE IMPRISONED AT HARD LABOR FOR NOT

MORE THAN 5 YEARS.

Below this sign is a bright yellow sign with the big red "stop" circle with a hand gun in the middle.

In many ways A.P. Toureaud looks like any other older American school: three story yellow brick, worn pebbled granite flooring on the entrance stairs, wide cement staircases from floor to floor, and worn wooden floors in the wide corridors and classrooms. The bulletin boards were covered with brightly colored Halloween and fall decorations. The asphalt playground is uneven, cracked and patched – I think of my elementary school playground in Virginia with large shade trees and soft green grass. There is some new equipment but not enough trikes or bicycles to go around. There's a large map of the United States painted on the asphalt in the three New Orleans colors – Massachusetts is purple and Louisiana is green. I show the children where Winchester is and how far I have flown to be with them.

The rusty chain link fencing around the school property has three layers of barbed wire at the top and only three houses on the block in front of the school are inhabited. The others are boarded up or gutted and wide open. They all share the prevalent Katrina red spray painted "X." In most cases the bottom quadrant has a zero painted there, which means no dead bodies of people or dogs were found inside. The top right quadrant says 9-11. It's hard to think that it has been well over two years since people have lived in their homes. One of the occupied houses has Christmas lights tacked around the "X." I hope they are celebrating inside.

My friend Patty and two other women made up the team of volunteers to work in the school for a week.. Each day we were "buzzed" into the large front doors and then entered through a metal detector that is monitored by a young, black, armed, woman security guard. After passing through four more doors, we entered the auditorium to face another armed security guard. No chairs in the auditorium, just a stage at one end and small, low sinks on the walls between the GIRLS and BOYS bathrooms.

We were assigned teachers and given a list of children. My teacher was Ms. Ferrand and some of my students were Richard, Samaiya, Destiny, Joseph, Jyrue, Diamond, Dajuan, Shequille, Victoria, Kentrell and Darriyanna. Samaiya is 6 years old, the rest were 5. Ms. Ferrand has twenty enrolled in her class – most days there are only 13 or 14 who actually attend.

As "tutors" we were given a piece of 8 ½ x 11 paper with large letter of the alphabet on it. Ms. Ferrand selected the children to come "study" with us. We have each child for 15 minutes – One on one. Our goal is to help the children recognize and know the sounds of the alphabet letters. Sadly, we discovered some second grade children don't know the alphabet letters by sight. I found an unused table and an old piano bench that I placed just inside one of the metal detectors. I called this area "Betsy's classroom." Diamond knew her letters and could write her first name but seemed to be confused when I asked her what her last name was. Ms. Ferrand told me it was because her mother had changed names for the second time earlier that week.

Lunch for my class was at 10:30 a.m. – this enabled all the children to get through the cafeteria by mid-day. It's well known that this may be the only hot meal for some.

As the children move about the building they must march in a straight line with a "leader" in the front who must always set a good example. There are always security guards nearby, and the children are positioned in line according to their height; this enables the teachers to determine if a child is missing. All children must wear navy trousers and powder blue golf-style polo shirts. There are no two alike in age or cleanliness.

On our third day, at about 10:30 a.m., I came out of the restroom to Patty's loud order of "Get down, get down – there's a man with a gun outside." I fell to my belly and crawled to where she and eighteen third graders were laying on their bellies. Some children were wide-eyed, some began to whimper, but most just lay there quietly. Patty and I lay head to head with the children's bodies perpendicular to ours. This made us the buffer for anyone that might have gotten through the lobby doors. In telling the story now, Patty says the children were "lined up like little match-sticks."

After 15 minutes of being horizontal, some of the children became bored and hungry. I began the first letter of an alphabet word game but it was not until after lunch that children assigned the word "gun" to the letter "G."

The "lock-down" lasted for twenty minutes, during which a teacher crawled the width of the auditorium to explain that there was a dead body in the street on the corner. A young man had been shot in the head and neck.

Finally the principal announced on the loud speaker that the school was once again safe and that we could resume our school activities. My class then marched quietly to lunch – cold Salisbury steak and mashed potatoes. Mrs. Ferrand wiped her eyes as she bent down to cut up the meat for her students. I had three bananas and two cartons of milk to settle my stomach. Social workers and counselors began to flood into the building and were busily seeking teachers who might need to talk. I saw several teachers crying.

Afterwards Mrs. Ferrand and I sat silently in the teacher's rocking chairs while Diamond and the other children lay in front of us on their little woven mats watching a Mickey Mouse cartoon on a tiny color television.

Classes were suspended early and the day ended with a Jazz Band Concert in the auditorium. The children sat cross-legged in rows, sometimes twenty-six deep, facing the stage. The leader of the four-piece band explained how we all needed to "dredge" up the events of the day. Then the children were instructed to stand up and from their tiny fists, they were to throw all their troubles to the floor. After the troubles were thoroughly stomped underfoot everybody danced to "When the Saints Go Marching In".

Toward the end of the day, the principal came on the loudspeaker again to assure the children that they were safe to leave the building and that they would be safe to return the next day. She thanked the teachers and said that they, along with the volunteers, were the real heroes of the day.

The school bus departures were rerouted away from the bloody corner and the good news was the children would return home unharmed.

We left the school in a sober mood, being thankful it was not our rental van that was riddled with bullets. As we pulled away, I heard the band playing "As the Saints Go Marching In" again.

Eight shots were fired on the corner of North Villere and Pauger Streets, and as a result Cardero Davis, age 20 of New Orleans, lay dead in the street. The New Orleans *Times Picayune* reported he was carrying a sawed off shotgun. It was also reported that the shooting was not school related and that all the children were safely in the building at the time.

Winchester feels very safe to me today. I wonder if the children of A.P. Toureaud feel safe. I wonder if they are being dropped off and picked up at the corner of North Villere and Pauger Streets again. I wonder what the children remember of the day they laid on their bellies playing ABC games with two white strangers. I'm reminded again of the senseless tragedies that repeat themselves over and over and over again in the ruins of New Orleans. I wish I could tell the boy's mother how sorry I feel about her son's death. I know the children don't stand a chance in hell of moving away from this is if they don't begin by learning their ABC's.

So, I've recorded this "dead horse" event and decided that it's time to "get off" of my constant remembrances of that day. After all, we were in the middle of the city – a very troubled city at best. Some think it's so troubled because all the grandmothers have left. They believe it was their influence that kept things sane.

I think if I'd been killed shielding those eighteen children it would not have been such a bad way to die.

I will return to A.P. Toureaud again in a few weeks. I wonder if the children will remember me and if Diamond will know her last name by then.

Later *The Times Picayune* offered a reward for information leading to the arrest of the two men seen leaving the corner in a white Toyota with no license plates.

November 12, 2007

SECTION V

WITH PAT

After a ten year relationship, Patricia Anne Meny and I were married on November 27, 2004 in the Winchester Unitarian Universalist Church by Rev. Mary J. Harrington

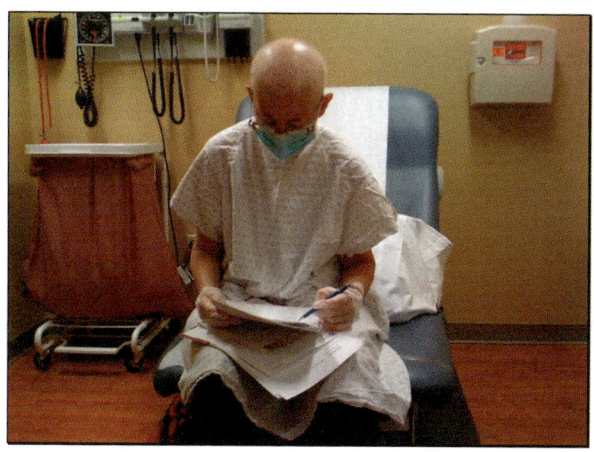

Unfamiliar

"We are mostly our true selves in unfamiliar places or around those who don't known.'

unknown

The alluring aroma of wet pines needles

in the woodland place, I know.

The forgiving cushion of leaves under foot and

the unforgiving rocks on the path, I know.

I am familiar with rainbow prisms that dance on your

skin from crystals hung in our bedroom window.

And I know the sounds of my dog as he stirs in his

sleep, chasing the playmates of his dreams.

Patients with caps and bandannas and magazines

named "Cope" and "Cancer 4 Living" are not familiar.

Single wrapped Oreos, Lorna Doone shortcakes and

Fig Newtons for extreme nausea are also new.

Syringes in our refrigerator and early morning shots

that stimulate stem cell growth are foreign.

Talk of white counts, nadir, suggestive vomiting and

different care-givers one after another is unfamiliar.

Our true selves are as brave in these strange places as we

were in breast cancer's unfamiliar place.

When we hear words like morbidity, survival and reoccurrence,

we are stronger than we ever knew we could be.

I want the familiar future we thought we knew;

when the dog is sweetly remembered and I am gone –

but not really.

Landmarks and Timemarks

Landmark: an object that marks the boundary of a piece of land.

A point of orientation. An important event or turning point.

Timemark: a time or happening that brings the reality of a situation closer.

A memorable event or realization.

All good paths and routes are peppered along the way with "landmarks." They are objects strategically placed to aid travelers as they try to find their way. I was guided for nine days by the image of a scallop shell as I walked The Way of St. James, a Pilgrimage which crosses Northern Spain to the western seacoast. There were stone pillars with the scallop shells carved into them, scallop shells painted on the sides of peasant houses and scallop shells forming an arrow cemented into the path.

There are strips of vivid orange tin nailed to trees along the Reservoir Trail in the Middlesex Fells Reservation in Winchester. These landmarks prevent Jack, our two year old Labradoodle, and me from losing our way on our daily walks.

On this leg of life's journey, I am guided and often alarmed by instances I now call "timemarks." Some are things that cause a low sinking feeling in the pit of my stomach or a sudden shiver that slaps me in the face with reality. Timemarks are making things much too real for me these days.

Opening our kitchen cabinet to find that some favorite crystal stemware had been replaced was a timemark. The thin etched pastel pink and lime green crystal juice glasses were gone. In their place were Hydrocodone, Alprazolam, Dexamethasone, Dapsone and Allopurinaol pills, a bottle of Nystatin, and two larger bottles of Acyclovir. A timemark that clearly indicated there is a sick person in the house.

Nineteen cards have replaced the family photos on our mantel above the fireplace. There is one with Snoopy, the Peanuts dog character, clearly under the weather. The sentiment reads "Wouldn't it be nice if life were like a DVD.... and you could fast forward through the crummy times?" Timemarks, although sometimes jarring, are helping us through our crummy time.

Our refrigerator now holds several plastic containers with taped labels on them. The handwritten messages describe the ingredients inside and there's a note on the kitchen counter indicating the weekly evening menus. These timemark containers, prepared by dear friends, are gifts of love and caring.

We are now forced to accept reality and we thank you for placing such meaningful timemarks along our path.

For Pat's
Care Group

Big Memories

In the summer of 1995 I lived and worked at the Maharisha's Ayurvedic Health Center in Lancaster, MA. People came to be treated for health issues or to spend time in meditation or silence. One of our weekly guests was a wealthy, truly gorgeous Asian woman. I guessed her to be about fifty years of age. She had brought her daughter to the U.S. on this visit because she wanted her to see the Statue of Liberty. The reasoning behind this was because, as she said very pointedly to me, "When first I saw it, as a young girl, it made a Big Memory for me."

I can think of several things during my life that have "made a Big Memory for me." Unfortunately, all the Big Memories are not pleasant.

There was a Christmas morning in Virginia when my brother Joey and I were probably five and nine years of age. Our four family members always had matching red-plaid pajamas for that special morning. Santa brought a beautiful ivory handled pocket knife to me and in a playful mood Joey held it by the blade to tap me on the head. I pulled the knife from his little hand and the blood flowed onto his special pajamas. We spent that Christmas Day at the doctor's office having the cuts in his little fingers stitched. It's a sad Big Memory for me.

I remember the 4th of July in 1976. Mickey Carlson and I had just started our small graphic design business. We worked seven days a week but this day was different – it was the centennial celebration and as we worked on her kitchen table, we watched the tall ships sail along the shoreline of New York City on a small black and white television. What a celebration of freedom and what a thrill it was for us to participate in the women's movement as entrepreneurs before it was time. Work has never been more fulfilling or sweeter. Remembering Mickey during that time makes a sweet Big Memory for me. Since 1976, we have our photo taken every ten years.

On November 27, 2004, the year same sex marriage was legalized in the state of Massachusetts, I walked down the main aisle of the Winchester Unitarian Church with Pat Meny to be married. We were the first lesbian couple to be legally married in that beautiful one hundred-year-old sanctuary. Our loved ones and friends threw fresh lavender as they cheered and clapped for us. Our minister Mary Harrington cried. Pat was very teary and promised in her vows to always be curious about me. The night after the wedding, I dreamt that my mother was smiling at me and clapping from an aisle seat on one of the middle pews.

The summer in 2009 is peppered with remembrances of Pat in light blue hospital Johnnies waiting in medical offices. I sat and watched her feet, often in striped socks and sandals, dangle from the exam tables. I also watched her read with her right arm extended while the chemo drugs entered her body. I always wondered what the next side effect would be and what our summer could have been like. These days made a Big Memory me.

Pat and I now have Village People. These are people who have moved toward us with open hearts and arms during this painful time in our lives. They have had dinner parties for us, taken the time to discover that I like Strawberry Fields cereal while Pat likes All-Bran. They have cooked and delivered meals to us – special foods for us, without cilantro. They have delivered homemade "medicinal chocolates." They have taken over the recycling and they've taken loving care of Jack when I could not. They have kept our home in flowers. These dear sweet people, will never know what a Big Memory they have made for me.

Thin White Hospital Blanket

Six of us sat there – two, two & two.

Steel lockers for our clothes made the fourth wall.

A small room, 8' by 8', if that,

but a huge air conditioning vent

blowing like a Northeaster overhead.

The frail, older woman had a worried look

under her full face of heavy make-up.

Slumped over – legs and feet drawn close together,

I waited for her to cry. I wanted to cry for her.

Next to me, a short and overweight woman,

maybe 40, in short shorts and dirty tennis shoes

was text messaging, looking for a sitter for her beagle puppy.

The youngest woman was quite thin. Dark roots
beneath her once dyed blonde hair.
She never looked up from her worn paperback book.
I bet she's been to this movie before.

The other two sat straight up with their purses on their laps
guarding their blank middle age faces –
no stories coming from them.
They passed the time in silence…
nervously looking at one, then the other, of the 4 of us.

In only worn blue print johnnies from the waist up,
we shared the chill of the room among other things.
A young aid took pity on our sorry looking lot and
passed out heated thin white hospital blankets.

I read "The Letters of Virginia Wolf" until it was my turn.
Anything to put me somewhere else.
"Just a regular mammogram on your right breast
but mammogram AND magnifications on your left…
we're following those calcifications."

Cold dim room, cold technician hands,

cold metal plates on the cold machine,

and the thought of having breast cancer again is cold.

Afterwards I take my seat again.

One by one we file in and out – then wait.

"No more calcifications, growing calcifications,

another mammogram, lumpectomy, mastectomy –" we wait…

I get an expressionless but fond farewell,

"Nothing new this time, you are free to go."

In the warm fall air of the hospital parking lot

suddenly I feel free – I feel light –

well, maybe free, maybe for six months…

or 12. It's the luck of the draw.

Remembering Karen Barton

She's got a ticket to ride, She's got a ticket to ride,

...and she don't care.

The Beatles

The silver is brought out from its blue velvet bags

...perhaps Karen had put it away.

Beloved solid pieces given to our congregation,

and she was given to us – for a short while.

A boom-box plays "She's got a ticket to ride."

It's Saturday morning. Some women sing along.

Gathered in the church kitchen around the large table

as we've done before – but with her here.

We set up familiar tables, our same wooden chairs.

We polish the silver and carefully cut squares of bread.

We make precise triangular sandwiches

…but she don't care.

Will people eat more egg salad than chicken salad?

Will they choose hot coffee or cold cranberry punch?

Should we use the new round glass or old oval platters?

…she don't care.

We discuss gender-equity, family vacations,

our next service trip to New Orleans,

dealing with the death of our parents

…but she's not here to speak.

She's left the silver, the sandwiches & the trivia

for a time we cannot fathom and

things we wish for and can only imagine.

And she was given to us – for a short while.

She's got a ticket to ride…and she don't care.

Virginia at Christmas

Bare cement and yellow construction tape

line the airport I used to know.

Gift laden, this time I wait on the curb.

Father and Mother, absent, are never closer

than when I am here. I want my blood, my people,

my childhood imagined perfect,

my guiltless sense of self.

Time has made their children older.

The boy more like his father.

The same soft sensitive ways.

I've mastered Mother's tenacity

while faltering in Fathers compassion.

Red brick houses hail the South, its

welcoming bull nose brick.

The dark verdant Magnolia contrasts

the light bark of the white Crepe Myrtle.

Mother preferred pink.

My tears wet the cotton sheets

on the Jenny Linn bed.

I finger the headboard distressed

by scratches from my great Aunt's diamond ring.

I picture her passion.

We dress in red and green flannel.

My nightwear waits on a slave-made chest.

Fresh pine underfoot, red holly berries

outside.

Mother, can you hear me?

My Autumn Life

Most solemn days, this season of my life

hovers over me

like the dull grey sky in January

hovers over our place on the bay

covering from every direction, inescapable

unforgiving.

My tired autumn body misses the

shape and feel of youth,

it whispers to me like blowing leaves

once green, now tan, once firm, now brittle

and curling.

I smell the damp dread of days to come

In pain, I am content to lie alone

I feel and taste the bitter brown leaves

remembering the green days, like ferns

when you loved my youth.

Yesterday, I fell backward

to the ground. Why can't I make that one tall step

From our beach to the path

like I did a million times,

strong without a thought,

in my wind-blown Spring?

The illusion of winter's bright light wakes me,

nudges me to hold tight against the chill,

to claim the next new seasons as mine,

to grab the yellow, blue and green once more

before brown comes again.

But again, I falter, reminded by the cold grey sky

strength was a green leaf of substance before,

balance was a green leaf of symmetry before

stability was a green leaf of resiliency before

spring was my life's season…before.

Memorial Service for 9/11, Boston's City Hall Plaza

With tear-streaked faces we stood,

Having never met, never to meet again.

We held each other's hands, September chilled.

Bette Midler sang "The Wind Beneath My Wings."

Twenty two doves were freed. They circled

then, at her last numbing note, disappeared

over the harbor into flawless sky

never to be seen again. The crowd

applauded with wet tissue-filled hands.

SECTION VI

BENEDICTION

Every day chain yourself to the tree of life

Everyday however desperate love one thing hard

Say to all with ears to hear, this life is a miracle every day

Rev. Mary J. Harrington

Written for her Installation as Senior Minister of the Winchester Unitarian Universalist Church

Winchester, MA

October 24, 2004

Watch and Learn

From Jackson Handsome "JACK" Bowles,

my six year old Labradoodle

3:29 a.m. –

my 88 lb. instructor lightly pads down the stairs

to find me.

I've been gone too long from our side of the bed.

He plops down, stretches his sleep tight muscles.

He allows his worried breath to yield

in his barely moving chest.

With closed eyes, he pictures himself romping

under the red sun, on silver-white sand by the bright blue bay –

He finds relief in sameness —

same red sun will surely reappear. Same walks by the same bright blue bay.

Same sweet, butter yellow treats, one inch square.

Surely light, white snow will fall and frost his beard again —

He silently counts the blessings of belonging

and recalls a sweet smile welcoming him home.

He treasures his very own bed — now shaped just like him

    -   And the best part, *believe it*,

God grows ice cream treats daily

on the bottom of the refrigerator door

Just for him.

Lily Pads in Beech Forest Pond

Voices must be left behind

Only chickadees are allowed to sing with the moan of God

A constant, maneuvering between the oaks

And in spring it blankets a hundred lady slippers

Sunrays sift through beech branches and hopscotch

patterns on the moss velvet ground below

Soft sacred ground not gut wrenching zero ground

No smoldering debris or charred beams as tall as oaks

I sleepwalk with the moan to the black pond water edge

Signature of the creator, a field of snow white lily blossoms

On another carpet green

The spiritual bodies of those who jumped that day

landing randomly, as snowflakes would, in a sacred place

They leave their voices in the sky

I wait, expecting them to rise up

together like the palms of my upward hands

Prayer and Meditation

On this day, may a heavenly spirit be with us.

May we begin anew with new strength, new creativity,

and new compassion.

May our worship and our work be vehicles for love.

Show us how to love deeply and to forgive.

Help us to withdraw our judgments,

our interpretations and our own agendas.

Show us the art of service filled with integrity.

May our presence be a blessing on others and on ourselves.

We dedicate our work to healing.

We take seriously this glorious mission in our hands.

We ask to be shown the way, now and forever.

Amen

ACKNOWLEDGEMENTS

Steve Gladstone (My friend from Jack's Pooch Play group) You introduced me to self-publishing, helped me with production, and mentored me through the process. Thank You.

Liz Bradfield (My teacher, reader and editor) You treated me like a poet and this book is far better because of you

Pat Meny (My Spouse) You filled me with love and enthusiastic support

Bertha C. Lipscombe (My Mother, 1918-2003) You funded this work in more ways than one

Cover: Original mud-head oil painting, "The Girl in the Orange Sleeves" Cape Cod School of Art, Provincetown, MA. Circa 1920 Artist Unknown

Pages 15 and 22: Original oil paintings by Michael Anne Carlson

Page 71: Photograph of Jackson Handsome "Jack" Bowles courtesy of Willey Peckham, Willey's Wild Life Photography

Made in the USA
Charleston, SC
02 February 2014